The giraffe is an African mammal with a very long neck and legs. It is the tallest land animal, often reaching a height of around 5 m (17 ft).

The great Mosque of Djenné in Mali is the largest mud structure in the world. Every year a fresh coat of mud is applied after the rainy season.

fascinating **facts**

The Sahara

The Sahara desert's boundaries are constantly shifting. As the climate becomes drier the desert continues to expand southward, making it impossible for farmers to sustain a living. Consequently there is a lot of poverty and starvation. The Sahara is the largest desert in the world. Many of its inhabitants are nomadic. People have to move frequently so their animals can forage for food as pastures become rapidly depleted in the dry desert climate.

The Tuaregs (a tribe of the southern Sahara) wear cloth around their faces to protect them from the sand. This is believed to originate from the belief that such action wards off evil spirits, but more probably relates to protection against the harsh desert sands.

Sahara desert

The Nile Delta

The fertile Nile Delta (a delta is the area where a river flows into the sea or a lake – often called the mouth of a river) is home to the densest population in Africa, i.e. Cairo and Alexandria. Cairo has a population of over 7 million and almost 4 million people live in Alexandria.

Kenya

Two tectonic plates have separated and formed this great valley which extends from Tanzania in the south, through the whole of Kenya and into Ethiopia in the North. Tectonic means that there is a structural deformation of the Earth's crust, such as the area is on an earthquake line. This area is still susceptible to earthquakes.

Coffee bush

Kenya is one of the most fertile countries in Africa. It is the third largest producer of tea in the world, and tea is a major source of the country's income. Tea is grown mainly in the Kenyan Highlands, west of the Rift Valley, and exports raise around £190 million ($350 million) each year.

Ethiopia

Ethiopia is the birthplace of coffee. More than 1,000 years ago, a goatherd in Ethiopia's highlands plucked a few red berries from the Kafa tree and tasted them. He liked the flavour, and the pleasant effect that followed. Today the same berries, dried, roasted and ground, have become the world's second most popular non-alcoholic beverage after tea. Coffee accounts for 63% of Ethiopia's exports and about 25% of the population depends on coffee for its livelihood.

Cairo

EGYPT

Khartoum

SUDAN

Asmera
ERITREA

DJIBOUTI · Djibouti
Addis Ababa

ETHIOPIA

SOMALIA

KENYA

Mogadishu

Kampala
UGANDA

Nairobi

RWANDA · Kigali

Kilimanjaro
19,341 ft
5,895 m

Bujumbura · BURUNDI

Dodoma

SEYCHELLES

CONGO
DEMOCRATIC
REPUBLIC

TANZANIA

COMOROS

INDIAN
OCEAN

ZAMBIA
Lusaka · Lilongwe

MALAWI

MOZAMBIQUE

MADAGASCAR · Antananarivo

MAURITIUS
Réunion (Fr)

Harare
ZIMBABWE

BOTSWANA

Pretoria
Mbabane · Maputo
SWAZILAND

LESOTHO
Maseru

Asia

Stretching from the frozen Arctic Ocean to the Equatorial islands of Indonesia, Asia is the world's largest continent. It contains the world's highest mountain – Mount Everest, on the border of Nepal and Tibet, 8,850 m (29,035 ft), as well as the world's deepest lake – Lake Baikal, which is located in Siberia, Russia, north of the Mongolian border, 1,637 m (5,369 ft) deep – that's more than 1.6 km (one mile) straight down!

Oil and gas

Asia is rich in natural resources, with over 75% of the world's oil and gas reserves. Russia has plentiful supplies of oil and gas, but they are difficult to source as they are under Siberia's frozen soil. Arabia has just 10% of the world's needs.

Forestry and agriculture

Forestry is extensive throughout northern and eastern Asia. Rice is grown in large quantities, and another main agricultural product is wheat.

Why do some women in Asia wear brass rings around their necks?

These women (right) are from the Padaung – part of the Karen tribe. There are many reasons given; some say it prevents them from being bitten by tigers; others suggest it makes the women unattractive so they are less likely to be captured by slave traders. But some believe that a long neck is very attractive.

Are all of the islands of Indonesia inhabited?

No. Approximately 7,000 of the islands are inhabited. They cover such an expanse of water that they spread over three time zones. Approximately 11,000 (61%) are uninhabited.

Over 600 languages are spoken in Indonesia, whilst Korea, on the other hand, is home to only one language.

A collection of over 8,000 life-size terracotta warriors and horses (below) was discovered in 1974 in the Shaanzi province in China. They had been buried with the first Emperor of Qin Shi Huang around 210–209 BC. Today they are known as the Terracotta Army. 700,000 workmen took 38 years to complete the work.

• Verkhoyansk

Vladivostock

ongyang NORTH KOREA

Seoul SOUTH KOREA

JAPAN
Tokyo

NORTH PACIFIC OCEAN

Taiwan

ong

PHILIPPINES

EI

ONESIA

Transport

The longest railroad in the world is the Trans-Siberian Railway, which connects Moscow with Vladivostok on the Pacific coast. It is 9,244 km (5,744 miles) long and the journey takes eight days. Shinkansen are the high speed trains in Japan, and they are known as bullet trains. The fastest Shinkansen train is the 500 series 'Nozomi' which operates at a maximum speed of 300 km/h (186 mph).

Bullet train

Island communities

The Philippines is an archipelago of 7,107 islands with a total land area of approximately 116,000 sq miles (300,000 sq km). An archipelago is a group or cluster of islands. The islands are commonly divided into three island groups: Luzon, Visayas, and Mindanao. The busy port of Manila, on Luzon, is the national capital. However, Indonesia has almost 18,000 islands! About 7,000 of these are inhabited, scattered around the equator, giving the country a tropical climate. The most populated island is Java (one of the most densely populated regions on Earth, where about half of the population of Indonesia lives).

Torii Gate

ndustry

he two most heavily populated countries in the world, hina and India, are in Asia; they are also the two fastest rowing economies. These countries and the huge area of e Russian Steppes are losing their communities as people ave the land to find work in the booming new industrial eas. There is an enormous contrast between the lives of the ch and those of the poor in this continent.

Manufacturing has traditionally been strongest in east and outheast Asia, particularly in China, Japan, Singapore, and outh Korea. The industry varies from manufacturing cheap bys to high-tech products such as computers and cars.

Environment

On August 6, 1945, towards the end of the Second World War, a nuclear bomb was dropped on Hiroshima, killing an estimated 80,000 people and heavily damaging 80% of the city. In the following months, an estimated 60,000 more people died from injuries or radiation poisoning. Since 1945, several thousand have died of illnesses caused by the bomb. The Torii (gate) to the Shrine at Miyajima on Itsukushima Island is much photographed by visitors to Hiroshima. Itsukushima Island is considered to be sacred.

The Chernobyl nuclear disaster in Ukraine in 1986 caused widespread devastation over a large area, and still the neighbouring towns are uninhabitable.

Australia

Australia is the largest island on the continent of Australia Oceania. Native Australians have inhabited it for over 42,000 years. European explorers and traders starting arriving in the 17th century and in the 18th century the British claimed part of the eastern half of the continent as a penal (prison) colony. This area became known as New South Wales. The population grew and eventually five more states were successively established over the course of the 19th century.

These were Victoria, Queensland, Northern Territory, Western Australia and South Australia. The island to the south of the mainland is Tasmania. On 1 January 1901, the six colonies became a federation and the Commonwealth of Australia was formed.

After the Second World War the Australian government promoted an immigration programme: over half of the migrants were British; others were Greek, German, Dutch, Italian and Yugoslav. Today over 90% of the population are of European descent; others are from Asia and the Middle East. Over 150 nationalities are represented in the population.

What is a flying doctor?

Australians living in the outback can be far from the nearest town. The Flying Doctor service started in 1928 to provide emergency health care.

Was Tasmania once joined to Australia?

Yes, it is believed that the island was joined to the mainland until the end of the most recent ice age, about 10,000 years ago.

Canberra is Australia's capital, but Sydney is its largest city and commercial centre, as well as having the world famous opera house and the 503 m (1,650 ft) long Sydney Harbour Bridge – which has eight lanes of roadway, two railway tracks, a cycle track and a walkway.

Sydney Opera House

The world's fussiest eater is the koala, which feeds exclusively on eucalyptus leaves. It eats only six of the 500 species of eucalyptus.

Although hunters have used throwing sticks in many parts of the world, the most famous of all such weapons is the Aborigine's boomerang, which may be the world's only returning throwing stick.

fascinating
Facts

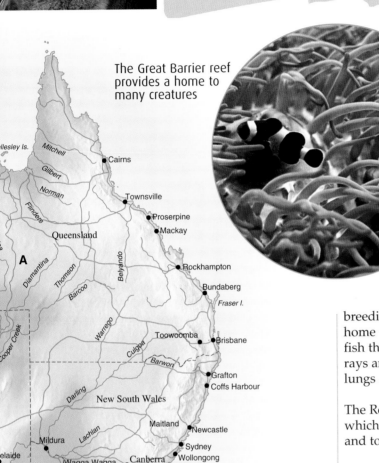

The Great Barrier reef provides a home to many creatures

Climate

While a large proportion of inland Australia is desert, 40% of the country enjoys a tropical climate. Snow falls in the Australian Alps at the south end of the Great Dividing Range, or Eastern Highlands. This is Australia's most substantial range of mountains, which stretches from north-eastern Queensland into the central plain in western Victoria.

The Great Barrier Reef

The Great Barrier Reef, situated off the coast of Queensland, is the world's longest reef, stretching 2,000 km (1,243 miles). It is a breeding ground for green and loggerhead turtles and home to humpback whales and dolphins. Among the many fish that inhabit Australia's surrounding waters are sharks, rays and lungfish. The lungfish is unusual because it has lungs as well as a gill-breathing system.

The Reef is under threat from the crown-of-thorns starfish which eats the living coral, and also from rising sea levels and tourism, which damage the fragile coral ecosystem.

Isolated communities

The Alice Springs School of the Air provides an educational service for children living in settlements and covers over 1 million sq km (386,000 sq miles) of central Australia. These children live in an isolated environment and their school classes were conducted via shortwave radio until very recently. Today most schools use wireless Internet links to receive their lessons.

Native Australians

The native Australians, known as Aborigines, were the first inhabitants of Australia. The term Aborigine includes a number of native peoples throughout Australia Oceania. These native Australians were hunter-gatherers; this means that they moved from place to place in search of food. They had no permanent buildings.

When the Europeans arrived they brought disease with them, and many of the native people died from illnesses such as smallpox. Today, many have abandoned their traditional tribal way of life and live in towns and cities, making up 1.5% of the population.

The regional headquarters of the flying doctor service in Queensland

Climate

W hen we talk about climate we generally mean the weather. Will it rain? Will it be hot or cold? How hot? How cold? But climate and weather are different.

Meteorology

Meteorology is the study of weather and weather conditions all around the world. Meteorologists can tell us about the temperature, rainfall and wind at any given place. They can tell us if there is likely to be a thunderstorm, a hurricane or flash floods. All of these factors make up what we think of as weather. Weather is what is happening now or likely to happen tomorrow or the next day.

Climatology is the study of climates and climate change. Climatologists can tell us what climate conditions to expect around the world. They are more interested in statistics – did it rain more in March this year than it did in March last year? And the year before that – and even in the last 50 years! The world has nine clear climatic zones. Each of the areas has a name, so that when we talk about a temperate climate or tundra, we know what to expect. For example, in the winter, we expect it to be mild and wet in Athens, Greece and snowy in New York, USA.

Forecasting

When we know all of these details we can judge if the climate around the world is changing. Are there more hot, dry days now than there were in 1950? Or does it rain more now than in 1950? If we know that, farmers will know which

Are there any places that never have rain?

There are places with very little rain or even no rain at all. The driest place recorded is Calama in the Atacama Desert in Chile, The average rainfall is just 3 mm (0.1 in.) per year, but there was a period of time when no rain fell there for 40 years.

Where is the wettest place ever recorded?

The wettest place recorded is Cherrapunji, India, where 9,300 mm (360 in.) of rain fell in one month!

ypes of crops to grow on their land. Water companies will
know if they need to make provision for water shortages.
Seaside towns will expect more people to visit the beaches.
Will the farmers be able to harvest their crops? Will there be
more floods? Where will we go for our holidays?

Types of climate

Mountain climate
Wetter than the lowlands and 1°C (2°F) cooler for
every 150 m (490 ft) increase in altitude.

Temperate grassland climate
Cold winters and warm summers. Mainly dry.

Temperate forest climate
Mild winters and cool summers. Abundant rain
falls all year.

Hot desert climate
Very hot and dry all year.

Tropical rainforest climate
Rainfall is heavy all year. The annual rainfall is often
more than 250 cm (100 in.). It is also hot and humid.

Coniferous forest climate
Very cold winters are common, with cool and mainly
dry summers.

Mediterranean climate
Hot dry summers and mild, wet winters.

Polar bear

Cheetah

Tropical grassland climate
Hot all year. Two seasons only – one dry and one wet.

Polar and tundra climate
Polar: dry and frozen all year. Tundra: dry and frozen
part of the year.

Desert life

A desert is a region that receives an annual rainfall of less than 250 mm (10 inches). The people and animals that live in desert areas must adapt to the conditions to survive. People like the Bedouins usually live in groups and move from place to place with the animals. Where there are homes in the desert, the houses usually have flat roofs and small windows. Whereas most animals need to have regular access to water, camels can survive for a week without water.

Deserts are generally rocky and bare and only partly covered in sand. Where there are large amounts of sand, the strong wind in sandstorms blows it into huge piles making sand dunes. It can then be very difficult for people to find their way as the landscape is constantly changing.

Desert plants

Plants which are found in deserts need very long roots to reach water underground, or thick stems which soak up water. Cacti can store water inside their stems and the whole plant swells up when it rains. In less severe conditions plants with leaves are often pale grey to reflect the light, and need very little water to grow. Seeds lie dormant during dry periods and grow and bloom and produce new seed very quickly when the rains come. In some places there are oases in deserts, where there is water. Palm trees often grow around an oasis.

Cactus

Desert animals

Many animals live in deserts, although they are rarely seen. As deserts are normally very hot during the day and very cold at night, most animals will only come out to hunt and find food at the cooler times of day, early in the morning or in the evening. Most desert animals are specially adapted to cope with desert life. Fennec foxes have huge over-sized ears to help them lose body heat quickly and easily. Sand grouse are very pale in colour, so well camouflaged and difficult to spot among the rocks.

Sand grouse

How many sorts of camels are there?

There are two types of camel: dromedary and Bactrian. The majority of the world's camels – about 15 million worldwide – are dromedaries with one fatty hump on their back where they store fluid. The less numerous camel is the Bactrian or Asian camel, which has a shaggier coat and two humps.

Llama

There are deserts on every continent on Earth. They are the driest places in the world and sometimes there is no rain for many years.

Llamas, which come from South America, are closely related to camels. They are also traditionally used for carrying goods and for their meat. Llamas are smaller than camels, weighing about 150 kg and measuring just over a metre in height.

How is sand made?

The extremes of temperature in deserts mean that the rocks are continually expanding and contracting in the heat of the day and cold of the night. This causes the surface of rocks to break off into tiny fragments, which become sand. As the sand is blown about, new rock surfaces are exposed and the process continues.

Lizard on cactus

Camels

How can camels go so long without water when other animals cannot? Although camels don't have to drink very often, perhaps only once a week, when they do drink they can consume as much as 100 litres at a time. That would be the same sort of quantity as half a tank of petrol in your family car.

Camels are often called 'ships of the desert' as they are used for carrying people and heavy loads of supplies across deserts. They are also used for the milk, meat and skin which they provide. Camels can grip very thorny food from plants with their tough lips and large teeth. In a sandstorm they protect themselves by pressing their ears flat, closing their eyes and sealing their mouths and nostrils almost completely. In this way they avoid breathing in sand or getting it in their eyes, which are protected by very long eyelashes.

Camel

Which is the world's largest desert?

The world's largest desert is the Sahara Desert in northern Africa. The Sahara covers nearly 10 million square kilometres (4 million square miles).

The European Union

The European Union (EU) is a group of democratic countries which have joined together. There are now 27 member states, and the EU has its own currency – the Euro. Not all of the countries use the Euro, preferring to keep their own currency.

Why a European Union?

Old frictions and rivalries between nations in the past led to instability or even war. Following World War I and World War II six European nations agreed to set up a group of countries within Europe who would work for permanent peace and also encourage trade between each other. They called themselves the European Economic Community (or the EEC or the Common Market). These first six countries were France, West Germany, Italy, Belgium, the Netherlands and Luxembourg. The name European Union came later because the purpose of the EEC changed from being simply a trading partnership into an economic and political partnership.

What has the EU achieved?

Since it was founded, the EU has:
• achieved over 50 years of peace in Europe
• helped to raise standards of living
• built a single Europe-wide market so that people, goods and money can move around as freely as if in one country
• launched the single EU currency, the Euro (€)
• strengthened Europe's position and voice in the world.

Which is the largest country in Europe?

By area France is the largest country, and Malta is the smallest. However, Germany has the largest population and again, Malta has the smallest.

Does the European Union have a president?

Yes. She or he is called the President of the Commission is selected by members of the European Council and is then approved by the European Parliament. The first president was Walter Hallstein from West Germany.

Euro notes are identical throughout the Euro area, while coins have a common design on one face and designs representing symbols unique to each country on the other face.

London, England, has the largest population of any city in the European Union, with over 7 million inhabitants. Berlin, in Germany, comes second with 3.5 million.

ARCTIC OCEAN

N

CZ.R.   CZECH REPUBLIC
LUX.   LUXEMBOURG
SLA.   SLOVAKIA
SL.   SLOVENIA

What if we didn't have the EU?

Try imagining a world now without the EU: we would still need to get our passports stamped when visiting nearby countries. We'd have to change our currency when we crossed from France to Spain. European businesses would be involved in constant negotiations when working with one another, without being able to look at agreed guidance and rules. Some of the poorer countries in Europe might not have benefited from trade partnerships and grants. And although countries might argue, we still have peace.

The European Parliament

A lot of people are needed to do all of the work that is carried out by the EU. The European Parliament represents around 450 million citizens. Its members are known as Members of the European Parliament (MEPs). Since the last European elections in 2004, there have been 732 MEPs.

Where is the European Parliament?

The parliament meets in two places – in Brussels and in Strasbourg – and the European Court of Justice is in Luxembourg. The European Bank is in Frankfurt. For three weeks of the month the parliament meets in Belgium's capital city Brussels, where most committee and political group meetings take place, then for one week everyone goes to Strasbourg in France. The Strasbourg Parliament on the border between Germany and France, which fought two world wars in the last century, is also a symbol of Europe's peaceful new order.

The current 27 member states:
Austria
Belgium
Bulgaria
Cyprus
Czech Republic
Denmark
Estonia
Finland
France
Germany
Greece
Hungary
Republic of Ireland
Italy
Latvia
Lithuania
Luxembourg
Malta
Poland
Portugal
Romania
Slovakia
Slovenia
Spain
Sweden
The Netherlands
United Kingdom

Mountains

A mountain is a landform that extends above the surrounding terrain in a limited area. This usually refers to landforms over 610 m (2,000 ft) in height. Mountains cover 20% of the world's land surface and more than half the world's fresh water originates in mountains. There are mountains on every continent, under the sea and even on Mars!

Mountains are formed over millions of years by volcanoes, erosion and disturbances in the Earth's crust. The Earth's crust is made up of six massive plates. When two of these plates collide, the land can be pushed upward forming mountains.

Kinds of mountain:

Dome mountains are formed when a great amount of melted rock pushes its way up under the Earth without folding or faulting; the result is a rounded dome. The dome is eroded as it is raised above its surroundings, forming peaks and valleys.

Fold mountains form when two plates smack into each other and their edges crumple. The Himalayas, Alps and Andes were created in this way.

Fault-block mountains are formed when faults in the Earth's surface force some blocks of rock up and others down. Instead of folding, the Earth fractures and the blocks are stacked. This is how the mountains of the Sierra Nevada in North America were formed.

Volcanic mountains form when molten rock ('magma') erupts from deep inside the Earth and piles up on the surface. Mount St Helens in North America is an example of a volcanic mountain.

Plateau mountains are plateaux (where land is flat) that have been worn down by erosion, and most have large areas of high-level flat land.

Mountain ranges

It is unusual for a mountain to stand alone – usually they exist as part of mountain ranges. A mountain range is a chain or group of mountains that are close together. The longest mountain range in the world is formed by the Andes Mountains, which are more than 7,200 km (4,474 miles) long. The highest mountain range in the world is the Himalayas (whose name means 'Land of Snow').

How are glaciers formed?

On the very coldest parts of some mountains, snow may build up and turn into rivers of ice that move incredibly slowly downhill.

Which is the tallest mountain in the solar system?

The tallest mountain in the solar system is Olympus Mons – on Mars!

Mountain climate

Mountains tend to be much wetter places than lowlands. They also tend to be colder – the higher you climb up a mountain, the colder it gets. This is why many mountains have snow on the top all year round, above what is called the snowline. Climate zones change quickly on mountains, so that one can climb from tropical jungle to the ice of a glacier in just a few kilometres (miles). The higher you climb, the lighter and thinner the air becomes.

Mountains can also affect local climates – in some areas, for example, they block rain, so that one side of the mountain may get plenty of rain but the other side is dry desert.

Mountain people

About 10% of the world's 6 billion people live on mountains. Eleven million people live in the Alps, making them the most densely populated

mountain area. Not only animals but humans as well have adapted to living in mountain environments – for example, the South American Uru tribe have larger hearts and lungs to help them breathe the thinner air at high altitudes.

Mountain animals

Mountains are a bleak habitat for animals; and the higher you get, the more bleak it becomes. Most mountain mammals have evolved thick woolly fur (like the yak), and mountain sheep and goats (like the ibex) are very sure-footed to help them on the rough terrain. Some of the highest mountain ranges are home to a variety of endangered species. For example, musk deer, Bengal tigers and snow leopards live in the Himalayas.

Mountain plants

The lower slopes of mountains are often covered with forest, while the tops of mountains are usually treeless. The place above which trees will not grow is called the treeline. Nevertheless, there are some plants that survive at very high altitudes where the terrain is mostly bare rock – mostly alpines, mosses and lichens.

Mountains and tourism

Over 50 million tourists head for the mountains each year. They are attracted by the clean air and beautiful scenery, and activities such as hiking, climbing, canoeing, skiing and snowboarding. Although tourism brings in money and creates jobs for mountain populations, there is also the risk that too much can do harm to the environment and local economy – through erosion, pollution from traffic, leaving litter, and raising the price of land and food.

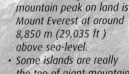

- The world's highest mountain peak on land is Mount Everest at around 8,850 m (29,035 ft) above sea-level.
- Some islands are really the top of giant mountains poking out of the sea!

Natural disasters

Throughout history there have been many natural disasters, the most deadly recorded as being droughts and famines. Floods are the next most deadly, followed by earthquakes and wind storms. Other deadly natural disasters include extreme temperatures, landslides, volcanoes and forest fires.

Hurricanes

One of the most damaging events is the hurricane, a fierce rotating storm with an intense centre of low pressure (the eye of the storm) that only happens in the tropics.

They are formed when large areas of the ocean become heated, and the air pressure drops. This causes thunderstorms and strong surface winds. As they travel long distances, gathering energy from the ocean, they are likely to be classified as strong tropical cyclones. A tropical storm can only be classified as a hurricane if it sustains wind speeds above force 12 on the Beaufort Scale.

Tornadoes

Tornadoes are caused by a collision of warm and cool air streams. A rotating area of low-pressure storm clouds forms, and air within a low-pressure front rises, creating a strong upward draught like a vacuum cleaner. Surrounding warm air is drawn in from ground level, causing it to spin faster and faster. These strong air currents can create a spiralling funnel of wind that can reach speeds of 483 km/h (300 mph).

Heavy objects, such as cars or even cows, can be sucked up and flung around like confetti. Many people have been killed in cars while they were trying to outrun a tornado, and although it is sometimes possible to escape, it is generally not a good idea.

Earthquakes

An earthquake is a tremor (shaking) of the Earth's surface. It is usually caused by the release of underground stress along fault lines. Fault lines, or faults, are rock fractures which show signs of movement. In spite of extensive research and sophisticated equipment, it is impossible to predict an earthquake, although experts can estimate the likelihood of an earthquake occurring in a particular region.

The point where the seismic activity occurs is the epicentre, where the earthquake is strongest. But it doesn't always end there because seismic waves travel out from the epicentre, sometimes creating widespread destruction as they pass.

Volcanoes

A volcano is formed when molten rock, called magma, explodes through the Earth's crust. Volcanoes vary in their structure – some are splits in the Earth's crust, some are domes, shields, or craters. When the magma bursts through the Earth's surface it is called lava. Sometimes ash and cinders come from the volcano, and also pumice, which is very light rock that is full of air bubbles and which can float on water.

Is a tsunami always caused by an earthquake?

A tsunami is caused by earthquakes, landslides, volcanoes or a massive impact, such as if a meteor crashed into the sea. Sometimes tsunamis have calmed down by the time they reach the shore; on other occasions they can be devastating.

What was the biggest known tornado?

In May 2004 in Nebraska, USA, the Hallam tornado became the record-holder for width, at nearly 4 km (2.5 miles). This is probably close to the maximum size for a tornado.

Tsunami

A tsunami is a chain of fast-moving waves caused by sudden trauma in the ocean. They can be generated by earthquakes, or volcanic eruptions. Tsunamis are also incorrectly known as tidal waves but, unlike tidal waves, they are not caused by changes in the tides.

As a tsunami leaves the deep water of the open ocean and travels into the shallower water near the coast, it is slowed down by the shallow water and its height grows. Tsunamis batter the coast with tremendous amounts of energy.

They are most common around the edge of the Pacific, where more than half the world's volcanoes are found. Over the deep Pacific Ocean, a tsunami travels at about 800 km/h (500 mph). If an earthquake happened in Los Angeles, a tsunami could hit Tokyo quicker than you could fly between the cities by jet.

Asian Tsunami

On Boxing Day 2004 the world witnessed the terrible power of one of the deadliest disasters in modern history. An undersea earthquake occurred about 8 a.m. local time. This triggered a series of lethal tsunamis that spread throughout the Indian Ocean. Waves up to 30 m (90 ft) devastated the shores of Indonesia, Sri Lanka, South India, Thailand and other countries.

10% of the world's population lives under threat from active volcanoes.

Often when an unusually destructive hurricane hits, that hurricane's name is retired and never used again. Since 1954, 40 names have been retired.

Hurricane Katrina (late August 2005) was the costliest and one of the deadliest hurricanes in the history of the United States. It was the sixth-strongest Atlantic hurricane ever recorded.

Fascinating Facts

Pacific Ocean

The Pacific Ocean is the largest ocean in the world, covering 65% of the Earth's surface. At almost 70 million sq miles (180 million sq km), it is considerably larger than the entire land area of the whole world!

The Pacific Ocean stretches from the Arctic Circle to Antarctica, and from the western coasts of North and South America across thousands of small islands to New Zealand, Australia, Japan and mainland Asia.

How deep is the Pacific Ocean?

The average depth of the Pacific Ocean is 4,637.5 m (15,215 ft) deep. At its deepest part, the Mariana Trench, it is 11,034 m (36,200 ft) deep.

Does the International Date Line change in the Pacific Ocean?

Yes, it travels roughly along 180° longitude, with diversions to pass around some countries or islands. The International Date Line is an imaginary line that separates two consecutive days. The date in the Eastern Hemisphere is always one day ahead of the date in the Western Hemisphere.

Peaceful sea?

Pacific is from the Latin words for 'Peace.' However the Pacific is not always peaceful. Many typhoons pound the islands of the Pacific. The area is full of volcanoes and often affected by earthquakes. Tsunamis, caused by underwater earthquakes, have damaged islands and destroyed entire towns and communities. Massive whirls, formed by ocean currents, are found in the area north and south of the equator.

Fishing

The main fishing areas in the Pacific are found in the more shallow waters of the continental shelf. The continental shelf is the extended land beyond each continent, which is relatively shallow. Then comes the continental slope, which eventually merges into the deep ocean floor. Salmon, halibut, herring, sardines and tuna are the chief catch. Not all fishing communities have large commercial fleets, however. Small island communities fish nearer to home.

Exploration and settlement

The first people who lived on the islands were from Asia. They crossed the open seas in ancient boats. Europeans explorers arrived in the 16th century, people such as Vasco Núñez de Balboa from Spain. During the 17th century the Dutchman Abel Janszoon Tasman discovered Tasmania

ASIA

BERING SEA

NORTH AMERICA

Sea of Okhotsk

Gulf of Alaska

Petropavlovsk

Aleutian Islands

Vancouver

Vladivostok

NORTH PACIFIC OCEAN

San Francisco

Seoul   JAPAN

Tokyo

Los Angeles

Yellow Sea

East China Sea

Tropic of Cancer

Tropic of Cancer

Hawaiian Islands

Philippine Sea

Is. Revilla Gigedo

Mexico City

San Salvador

San José

Manila

MICRONESIA

Marshall Is.

Clipperton I.

Caroline Is.

Gilbert Is.

Bogotá

Equator

MELANESIA

Nauru

Kiribati

Line Islands

Kiritimati

POLYNESIA

Galapagos Is.

SOUTH AMERICA

INDONESIA

Phoenix Is.

Lima

Port Moresby

Solomon Is.

Tuvalu

Tokelau

Îs. Marquises

Vanuatu

Wallis & Futuna

Western Samoa

Coral Sea

Fiji

Tonga

American Samoa

French Polynesia

New Caledonia

Niue

Cook Is.

Tahiti

Îs. de la Société

Îs. Tuamotu

AUSTRALIA

S.Fiji Basin

Îs. Tubuai

Îs. Gambier

Tropic of Capricorn

Great Barrier Reef

Brisbane

Norfolk I.

Pitcairn

Sala y Gómez

San Félix

Sydney

NEW ZEALAND

Easter I.

Îs. Juan Fernández

Santiago

SOUTH PACIFIC OCEAN

| 0 | 600 | 1200 | 1800 | 2400 miles |

Tasman Sea

Hobart

Wellington

| 0 | 1000 | 2000 | 3000 | 4000 kilometres |

...d New Zealand. Then the 18th century saw the Russians ...nd in Alaska, and the French settle in Polynesia. The ...ritish sailed with Captain James Cook to Australia, the ...uth Pacific, Hawaii, and North American.

...uring the 1800s Charles Darwin's ...search on his five-year voyage on the ...MS Beagle brought him fame as a ...eologist and author. He studied the theory ... evolution and natural selection.

In 1859 he published the book *On the Origin of Species*. Many of the animals he studied can still be seen in the Pacific, in particular the turtles and tortoises of the Galapagos Islands.

The Pacific is rich in mineral wealth, but the ocean is so deep that mining would be very difficult and dangerous. In the shallower waters of the continental shelves off the coasts of Australia and New Zealand, petroleum and natural gas are extracted, and pearls are harvested along the coasts of Australia, Japan, Papua New Guinea and the Philippines.

fascinating facts

90% of all volcanic activity occurs in the oceans.

If you placed Mount Everest in the Marianas Trench there would still be over 1.6 km (a mile) of ocean above it.

19

Seashore *and* coastal erosion

We usually picture sandy beaches when we think of the coast, but actually a coast is any land that borders the sea. The place where land and sea meet is usually called the shoreline or seashore.

Beaches

A beach is a sloping area of sand, pebbles or shingle along the very edge of the sea. Most beaches are made of sand, though some are rocky. Some are even made from broken seashells! Rock pools are pools of sea water that are trapped in rocks on the beach when the tide goes out, and are home to a wide variety of tiny wildlife.

Coastline features:

Bay – A bay is a wide indent in the coast, between two headlands. Bays are usually sheltered spots. A small bay is called a cove. A huge bay is called a bight, and a gulf is a long, narrow bight.

Cliff – Cliffs are formed over millions of years by waves wearing away the edge of the land.

Estuary – An estuary is an area where the mouth of a river widens out and meets the sea coming in, causing fresh and salt water to mix.

Headland – These are long 'tongues' of land sticking out into the sea. Headlands are created over millions of years, as waves strike rocky shores, wearing away the softer kinds of rock and leaving the harder ones.

Spit – Also called sandbars, spits occur when sand and debris are washed out across bays by waves, creating 'tongues' of sand that run out into the sea.

Features created by coastal erosion

The coastline is always changing, very slowly, due to natural processes like the rise of sea levels, the pounding of the waves, and weather. In most cases, the result is that the coast is gradually being worn away. We call this wearing away erosion. Coastal erosion can create many spectacular features in places where the coast is made up of different types of rock.

Sea caves are formed when waves wash away an area of softer rock at the base of a cliff, making a hollow inside harder rock.

Sea arches like the one top right are produced when two sea caves are worn away from different directions and then meet when the rock separating them is worn away.

Q&A?

Why does seaweed float?

Seaweed needs to be on or near the sea's surface because further down in the water there is not enough light for it to thrive. Seaweed uses trapped air in 'pods' to make it float.

How is sand produced?

Sand is produced as waves grind down rocks and cliffs into smaller and smaller pieces.

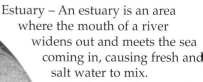

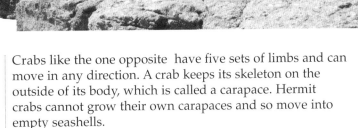

Sea stacks like the one below are formed from sea arches, when erosion finally causes the top of the arch to collapse. This leaves only a pillar of rock standing alone in the sea.

What lives on the seashore?

Sea anemones like these above are brightly coloured creatures that look like flowers when the many tentacles that surround their mouths are extended. These tentacles are used to capture prey and to sting anything that attacks the anemone. They have no skeleton and can only move very slowly.

Starfish have no bones. Most have five arms – if an arm is cut off, the starfish will grow another! Their mouths are underneath their bodies – a starfish that wants to eat especially large prey can actually push its stomach out of its mouth to catch and digest the prey.

Sea urchins are spiny, hard-shelled creatures which are often found washed up on beaches. They have spines all over their shell for protection, and some urchins have venomous spines.

Crabs like the one opposite have five sets of limbs and can move in any direction. A crab keeps its skeleton on the outside of its body, which is called a carapace. Hermit crabs cannot grow their own carapaces and so move into empty seashells.

Limpets are shellfish with flattened, cone-shaped shells. They have a muscular 'foot' which allows them to seal themselves to the rocks and cling on to avoid being washed away by the tide.

Shellfish such as mussels, clams and winkles live inside shells and attach themselves to rocks with the 'foot' underneath the shell. Many shellfish are edible.

Seaweed

The UK and Ireland together have 13,870 km (8,618 miles) of coastline.

Sea anemones can live for up to 100 years!

Coral is built from skeletons of tiny animals called polyps. Polyps use their tentacles to capture food by special stinging cells in their tentacles that numb their prey. Then the tentacles pass it to the polyp's mouth.

fascinating facts

United Kingdom

The United Kingdom comprises Great Britain and Northern Ireland. Great Britain is Europe's largest island and for the last 500 years has been one of the world's most influential and riches countries. At its height the British Empire stretched over 25% of the Earth's surface, ruling countries such as Canada, South Africa, India and Australia, which is why so many nations in the world speak English. The Empire is no more, and Scotland, Wales and Northern Ireland now have their own parliaments.

The UK was a world leader in shipbuilding, steel making, car manufacturing and coal mining, but these have declined, with most people now employed in finance, health care, education, retail and tourism.

Languages

The language of the UK is predominantly English, although Welsh is spoken by 25% of the Welsh people and Gaelic is spoken to a lesser extent in Western Scotland and the Hebrides. Cornish is spoken in small areas of Cornwall. The UK is a multi-cultural society and many languages are spoken, mainly from the Indian subcontinent and Africa.

England

England is the largest of the British nations and has, in London, one of the most cosmopolitan capital cities in the world. It is home to both the government and the

monarchy and the headquarters of many national institutions and companies. This combination of royalty and national monuments attracts tourists from around the world. The most visited sights are Westminster Abbey, Downing Street and St Paul's Cathedral.

Northern Ireland

Northern Ireland consists of the six counties of Ulster and i situated in the north-east of Ireland. It covers 14,139 sq km (5,459 sq miles), about a sixth of the total area of the island. It is mostly rural with industry centred around the capital Belfast.

Northern Ireland's most spectacular feature is the Giant's Causeway (a causeway is a path). The unique rock formations have withstood Atlantic storms for millions of years. This feature is the result of volcanic activity. The Causeway itself is made up of hexagonal columns of differing heights. There are over 40,000 of these columns. The story is that the giant stepped from Ireland and over to Scotland, using the columns on Staffa (near Mull in the Scottish Highlands) as a stepping stone.

Giant's causeway

Was the Titanic built in the UK?

The Titanic was built at the Harland and Wolff shipyard in Belfast, Northern Ireland. She was the largest passenger ship in the world. On April 14, 1912, she broke into two pieces, and sank two hours and forty minutes later at 2:20 a.m. Monday morning.

Why doesn't the Queen rule England?

England (and the rest of the UK) has been ruled by a parliament of elected officials since the mid-13th century.

representatives who have total control over issues such as education, health, agriculture and justice. The parliament is in the capital city of Edinburgh, which has many fine buildings such as Edinburgh Castle and Holyrood House.

Wales

Successive English Kings tried to integrate Wales into England. King Edward I ordered a ring of castles to be built to circle the land but it was not until the reign of Henry VIII that Wales was fully intergrated. The castles today remain as magnificent tourist attractions. Wales is a rugged country; in the north are the magnificent mountains of Snowdonia. Mid Wales has a more rolling countryside but is very sparsely populated, while in the south are the Black Mountains and the coal-rich Welsh Valleys. It is in this region that the capital, Cardiff, is situated and where most of the people live.

Scotland

The Celts of Scotland have always fiercely defended their homeland. The Romans could not defeat them and built two walls, the Antonine Wall between the River Clyde and the Firth of Forth and Hadrian's Wall between the River Solway and River Tyne, to try and keep them out of England. The two countries became unified in 1707. The Scots achieved their own parliament in 1998 and elected

Stonehenge is a megalithic monument located in the English county of Wiltshire. It is composed of earthworks surrounding a circular setting of large standing stones and is one of the most famous prehistoric sites in the world. Archaeologists think thestanding stones were erected between 2500 and 2000 BC.

Britain is the home to the world's most poisonous fungus, the yellowish olive Death Cap.

Fascinating Facts

The USA

The USA stretches from the Arctic Ocean to tropical Hawaii and includes the massive Rocky Mountains as well as fertile lowlands. Vast natural resources and a culture of enterprise make the USA one of the world's richest nations, the home of many global businesses such as Ford, McDonald's, Microsoft and Disney.

The people

The United States has one of the world's most diverse populations, with immigrants from all over the world. Thousands of years ago, Asians crossed the Bering Strait from Asia and populated both North and South America. Their descendants are the Native Americans. Spanish, French and English settlers colonized in the 1600s, and slaves from Africa were brought to the country later. The Industrial Revolution attracted millions of European immigrants from Ireland, Britain and Italy, and the last 50 years have brought immigrants from Mexico.

Western USA

Here the nation's most dramatic landscapes can be found. The Rocky Mountains form several large mountain ranges. Vast quantities of powder snow make this one of the world's biggest winter skiing areas, the main centres being

near Aspen in Colorado and Lake Tahoe in California. As the traditional coal, steel and automobile industries of the Eastern USA declined, many people moved to the West Coast where new industries were growing. Aircraft and software development in Seattle, computer component development and manufacture in 'Silicon Valley' San Francisco, and the music, movie and entertainment industries of Los Angeles have built one of the richest regions in the world. Television and film dominate American culture and spread it throughout the world. Hollywood movies are viewed worldwide, as are such long-running television programs as 'The Simpsons'.

Southern California, Nevada and Arizona are desert, the driest place being in Death Valley. Water from the River

What do the stars and stripes mean on the United States flag?

The flag of the United States has 13 horizontal red stripes, which represent the 13 original colonies. In the top left corner of the flag is a blue rectangle with 50 small, white stars. These represent the 50 states in the United States of America. The flag is known as 'the Stars and Stripes'.

Did the Mayflower take the first settlers to America?

No. The first settlers are thought to have been a group of English traders who landed in Virginia in 1607. But the Mayflower, which sailed in 1620, is probably the most famous of the early ships to go to America. Those on board included 102 passengers from Holland and Britain. A replica of the Mayflower can be seen at Plymouth, Massachusetts.

...Colorado has cut the deep gorges of the Grand Canyon and Bryce Canyon, and provides much needed water for the farmers and cities of California.

Eastern USA

Europeans have settled the eastern half of the USA since 1613, and many towns are named after the places from which these colonists came. People who migrated to settle permanently in colonies controlled by their country of origin were called colonists or settlers. Sometimes the settlers formed the colony themselves if they settled in an unpopulated area. A colony is the territory where the people settle.

New Orleans

New Orleans, called the Big Easy due to its relaxed life style, is the world's jazz capital, and the Mardi Gras festival attracts millions of visitors. In August 2005, Hurricane Katrina, the largest hurricane ever recorded over the USA, flooded over 80% of New Orleans.

Washington, D.C.

Washington, D.C., named after the first President, George Washington, is the capital city and home to the President of the United States and to the US Capitol. It was designed in 1791 by a French architect and was the world's first planned capital. Washington, D.C., is one of America's most visited sites.

The world's largest silver nugget, weighing 835 kg (1,840 lbs) was found in 1894 near Aspen, Colorado.

Disney World, near Orlando, Florida is the world's largest tourist attraction, covering an area of 12,140 hectares (30,000 acres).

Fascinating Facts

Volcanoes

Deep under the Earth is very hot runny liquid called 'magma'. Sometimes the magma rises to the surface, building up great pressure, and than an eruption occurs. When this happens, a volcano is formed. Gases and lava shoot up through the opening and spill out, causing lava flows, mudslides and falling ash. Large pieces of lava are called lava bombs. An erupting volcano can also cause earthquakes and tsunamis.

Active volcanoes

A volcano is considered 'active' if lava comes out of the top. When this happens, the volcano is 'erupting'. If volcanoes have been quiet for a long time they are 'inactive'. Some inactive volcanoes suddenly become active.

Dormant and extinct volcanoes

Some volcanoes have not erupted for at least 10,000 years. These volcanoes are described as dormant, since they have the potential to erupt again. Some volcanoes only erupt once, and these are called 'extinct', because they will not erupt again.

Cone shapes

The volcano's eruptions can create cone-shaped accumulations of volcanic material. The thickness of the underground magma determines how a volcano will erupt, and what kind of cone will form. There are three cone shapes: cinder cones, shield cones, and stratovolcanoes cones.

Cinder shapes

Cinder cones have straight sides with steep slopes and a large, bowl-shaped crater at the summit. They rarely rise to more than 304 m (1,000 feet) above the surrounding landscape. They are known for their very violent, explosive, exciting eruptions. Paricutin in Mexico is a famous cinder cones.

Shield shapes

Shield cones have very gentle slopes. They were named by Icelandic people because the cones' shape reminded them of a warrior's shield laid down. These volcanoes erupt many times over the same area forming huge, thick lava plateaus. The Columbia Plateau of the western United States is the largest lava plateau in the world. It covers almost 259,000 sq km (100,000 square miles) and is almost a mile thick in places.

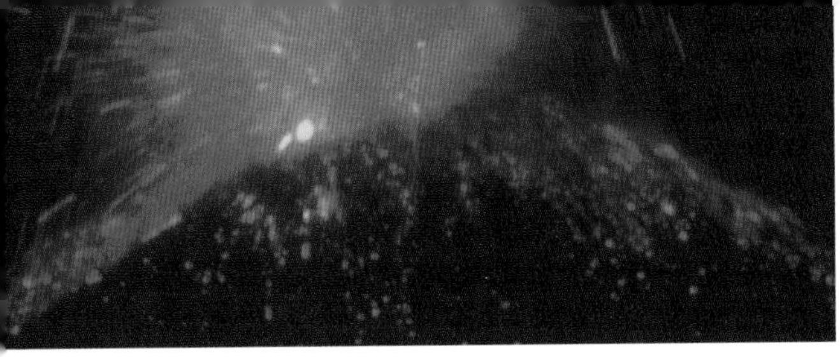

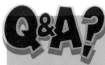

·tratovolcanoes shapes

:ratovolcanoes cones have gentle lower slopes, but steep ɒpper slopes. They are formed from a combination of ·uptions. First the volcano has an explosive eruption that ects huge amounts of steam, gas and ash. This is followed y the ejection of lava. A large cone is built up with many yers of ash and lava. These are the most common volcanic cones, and a famous example is Mount St Helens in Washington.

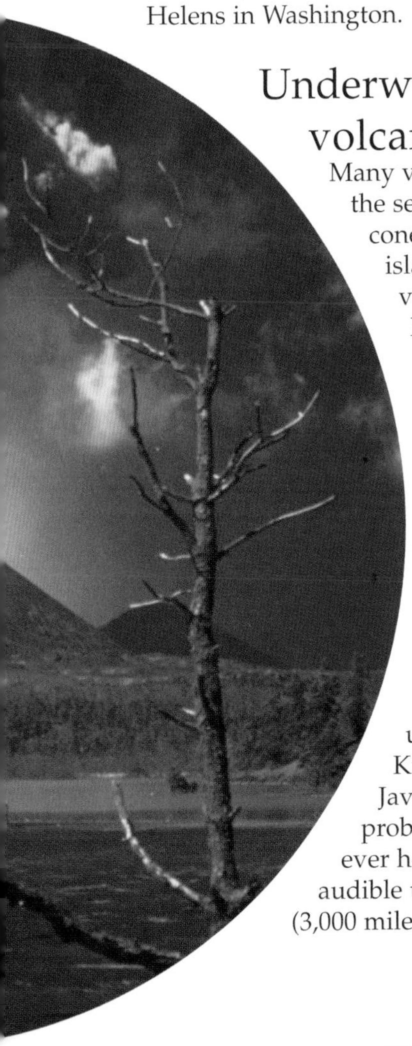

Underwater volcanoes

Many volcanoes begin on the sea floor. The vast cones of the Hawaiian islands and many other volcanic islands in the Pacific Ocean began like this.

Worst eruptions

There have been many cataclysmic eruptions. After a series of eruptions over the course of several days (26–27 August 1883), the uninhabited island of Krakatoa in Sumatra/Java exploded with probably the loudest bang ever heard by humans, audible up to 4,800 km (3,000 miles) away. About 200,000 people died, most of them killed by subsequent tsunamis with waves up to 30 m (98.5 ft).

When Vesuvius erupted suddenly in 79 AD, the town of Pompeii in Italy was buried under a vast layer of rock and volcanic ash. The town was preserved in a near-perfect state, and uncovered by archeological excavations that began in 1738.

Q&A?

How often do you think volcanoes erupt?

Every day, ten volcanoes erupt somewhere on Earth. Most of these are small eruptions, but they may be followed by larger ones.

What is 'The Lighthouse of the Mediterranean'?

Stromboli, off the coast of Italy, has erupted repeatedly over many centuries. The volcano has been called 'The Lighthouse of the Mediterranean' because it erupts every 20 minutes or so.

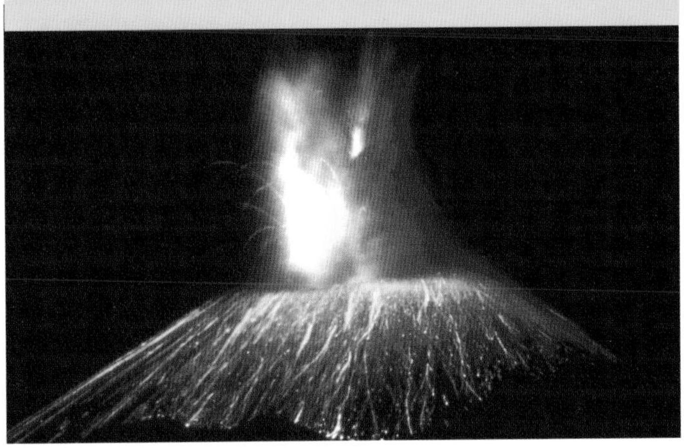

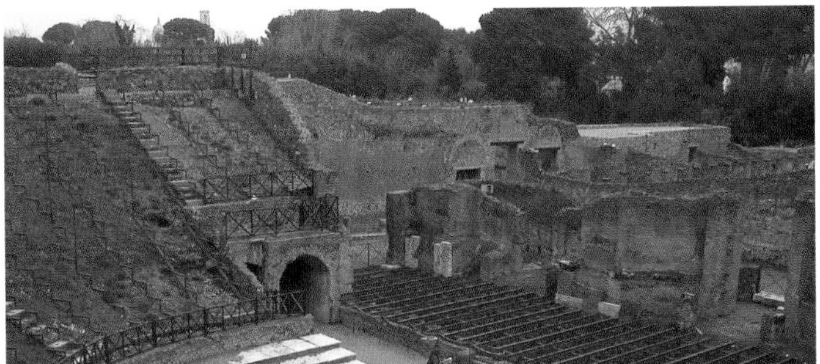

Fascinating Facts

The word volcano comes from the Roman god of fire, Vulcan. Vulcan was said to have had a forge (a place to melt and shape iron) on Vulcano, an active volcano on the Lipari Islands in Italy.

Mauna Loa, Hawaii, is the tallest mountain in the world if measured from the floor of the ocean where it was formed. It is 4165 m (13,677 ft) above sea level, but over 5177 m (17,000 ft) lies under the water. So this volcanic mountain is over 9137 m (30,000 ft) tall!

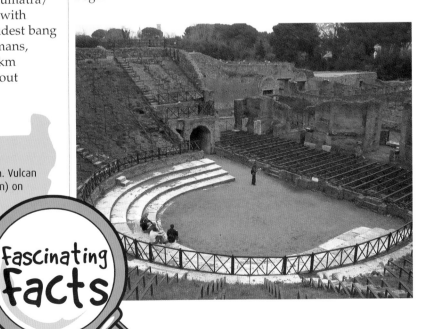

Wilderness

W e usually think of wilderness as an area of land unchanged by people. Many areas of wilderness or near-wilderness exist around the world and form an important part of the Earth's ecosystem. An ecosystem is a unit consisting of a community of organisms and their environment. For example, a pond is an ecosystem with plants and animals that depend on each other for survival.

The word wilderness comes from the Old English 'wildeornes', which means wild beast.

Throughout history, the majority of our planet has been wilderness, because humans only settled in particular areas. However, in the 19th century it was realised that wild areas in many countries were disappearing fast, or were in danger of disappearing. This led to the creation of a conservation movement, initially in the United States, to reduce the impact of human activity on the landscape.

The Wilderness Act

The United States passed The Wilderness Act in 1964, which designated certain areas of land as 'wilderness'. This provided the first official protection for wilderness areas, although there had been ideas about protecting them much earlier in the 20th century. The Wilderness Act restricts the building and leisure activities that can take place in these areas, which help to conserve the animals and plants that live there. There are a wide variety of wilderness areas, some being mountainous whereas others are wetlands.

National parks and forests

Many countries have national parks and forests where human activity is limited. Whilst some people may live and work in the area, there are very strict rules about building and industry. There is often limited farming in these areas and people are encouraged to visit them to pursue leisure activities such as walking, mountain-climbing or water sports.

Hunting reserves

In many areas of the world, wildlife reserves have been set up to conserve animals just so that they can be hunted. This is how many of the big game reserves in Africa first came into being. However, ideas of making areas into natural hunting reserves date back much earlier, to the hunting reserves created by the kings of England in the Middle Ages.

n the UK the oldest nature reserve is Wicken Fen in Cambridgeshire, a vast wetland area which was established in 1899. The fens have been changing since Roman times, and this area was the only part which remained of the original landscape.

What is the oldest national park in the world?

Yellowstone National Park in the US.

In what year was the WorldWide Fund for Nature (World Wildlife Fund in the US) formed?

1961.

WWF

Wilderness is the name of a city in South Africa.

The first nature reserve in the world was in Sri Lanka in the 3rd century BC.

More than 10% of the Earth's land mass is a nature reserve or a recognised wilderness area.

Nearly 5% of the land in the US is designated as wilderness, but more than half of this is in Alaska.

Countries

Largest countries

17,098,242 sq km (6,601,668 sq miles) Russia

9,970,610 sq km (3,849,674 sq miles) Canada
9,629,091 sq km (3,717,812 sq miles) United States of America

9,598,086 sq km (3,705,841 sq miles) China
8,514,877 sq km (3,287,612 sq miles) Brazil